GOD HAS A PLAN FOR THIS

Amanda McKinney

ISBN 979-8-88685-918-8 (paperback)
ISBN 979-8-88832-513-1 (hardcover)
ISBN 979-8-88685-919-5 (digital)

Copyright © 2023 by Amanda McKinney

All rights reserved. No part of this publication may be reproduced, distributed, or transmitted in any form or by any means, including photocopying, recording, or other electronic or mechanical methods without the prior written permission of the publisher. For permission requests, solicit the publisher via the address below.

Christian Faith Publishing
832 Park Avenue
Meadville, PA 16335
www.christianfaithpublishing.com

Printed in the United States of America

To my inspiring husband, Tyler, and our exceptional children. Thank you for allowing me to share part of our story in hopes that it will help others who are walking the lonely journey of heartbreak and loss. May we all forever hold our little one's memory in our hearts and cling to the promise that God has a plan for this.

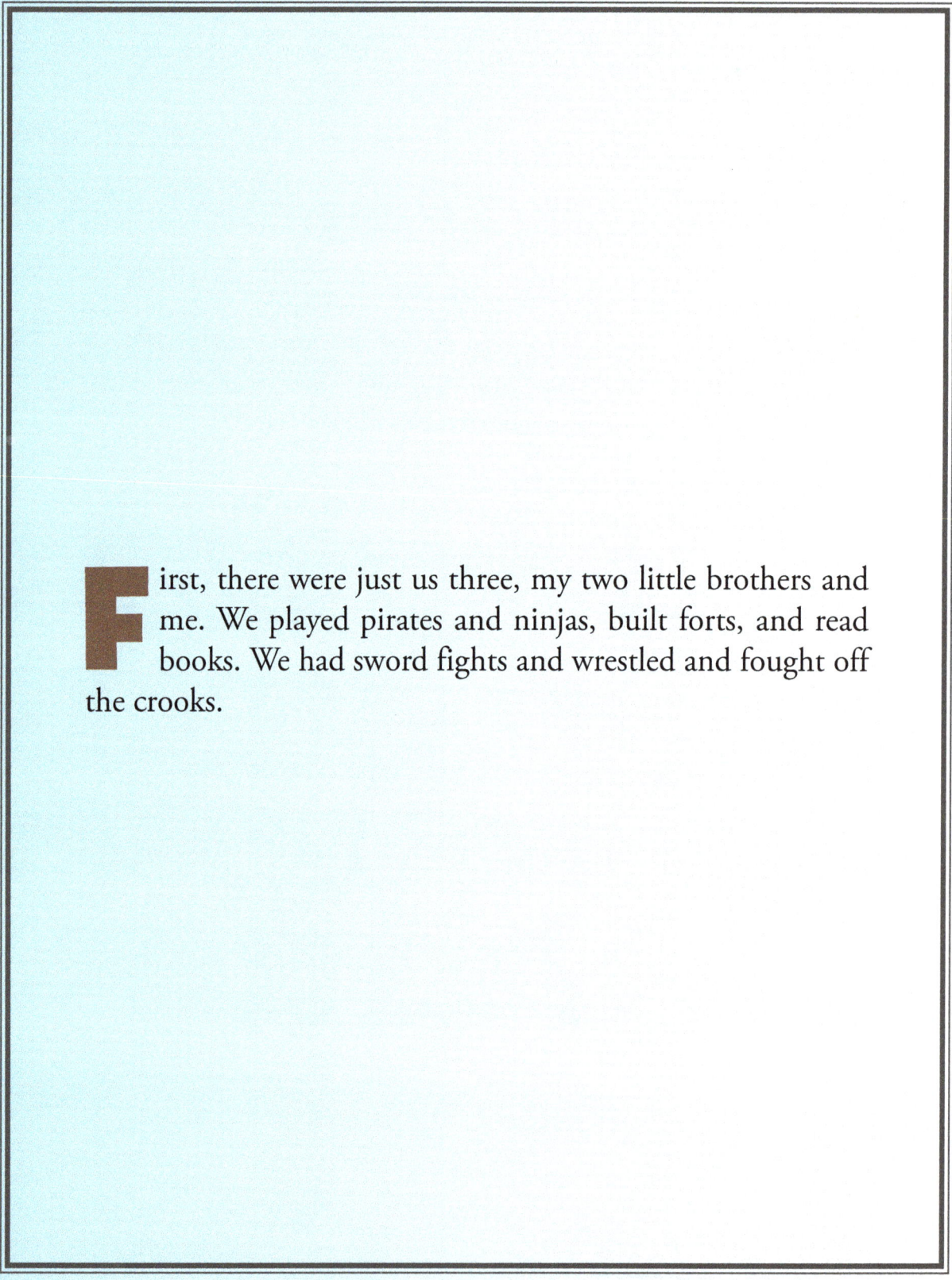

First, there were just us three, my two little brothers and me. We played pirates and ninjas, built forts, and read books. We had sword fights and wrestled and fought off the crooks.

I have so much fun with my brothers, you see, but it is hard to have teams with just us three.

We need another kid to be in on our games. Maybe Novah or Samuel, Parker or James?

Who could we find to fill in that gap? Maybe I'll think about it during my nap.

Then one day, Mommy and Daddy said they had a surprise we'd adore. They said that Mommy was having a little baby, and that would make *four*!

Mommy showed us her tummy and looked down with a smile. She told us that the baby would be there awhile.

They leaned in close to give us a kiss, and I jumped for joy because I was getting my wish!

I gave them a hug and said, "Hey," to the baby.

Then I ran out to play and thought, *It could be a sister, MAYBE!*

I talked about her all the time, and I even practiced all my silly nursery rhymes.

I'm a really-great big brother; it's true, but there was still a lot of practicing I had to do.

Then one day, Mommy said she didn't feel very good, and Daddy took her to the doctor as fast as he could.

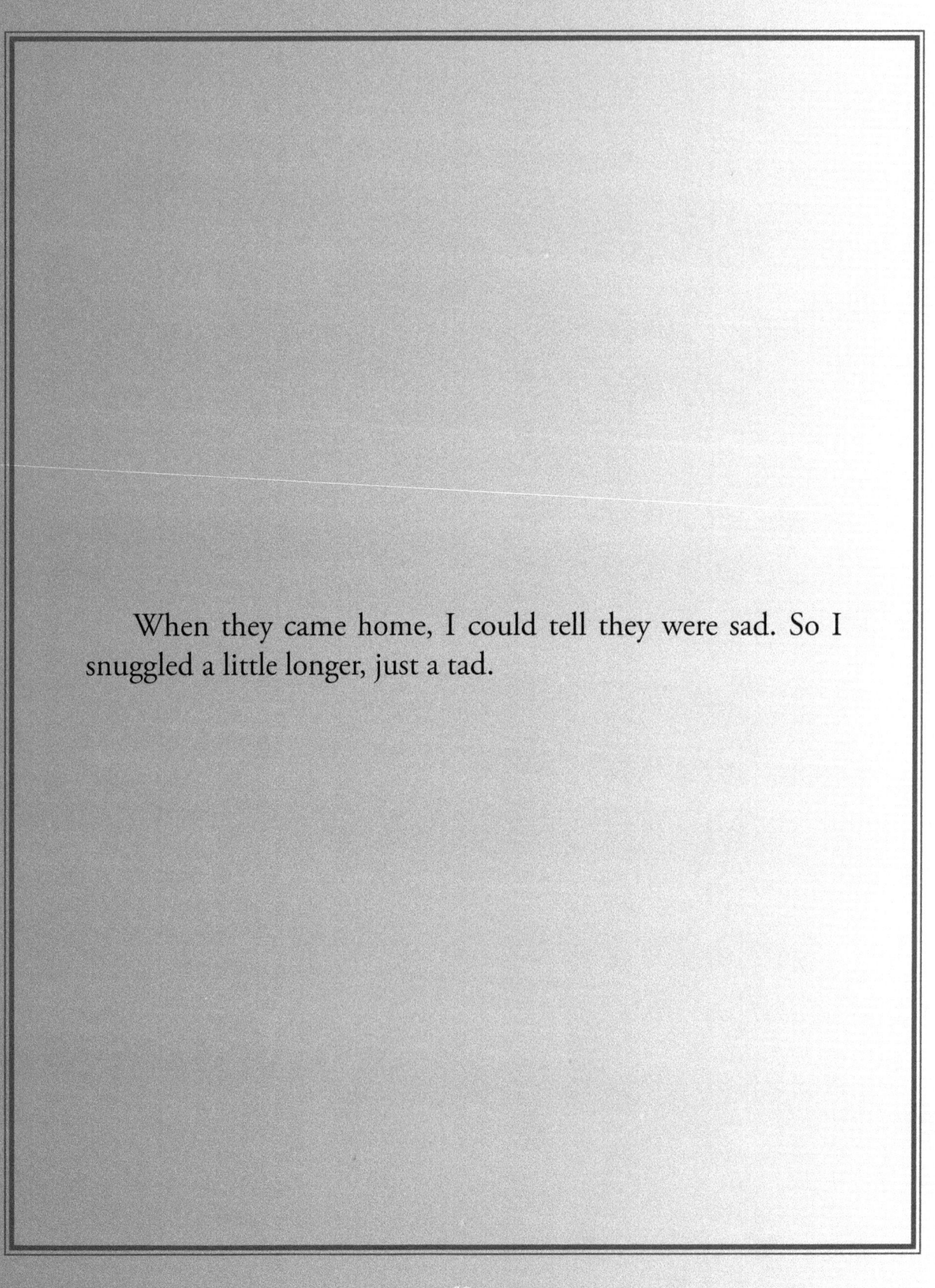

When they came home, I could tell they were sad. So I snuggled a little longer, just a tad.

Daddy told us that the baby in Mommy's tummy was sick and would be going back to heaven. I wish this was a trick.

Later, I sat with my mommy and asked her, "Why?" She hugged me really tight as we both started to cry.

She told me that sometimes, God sends a baby our way to put a little more joy in our day.

And sometimes, God brings that little baby back because He has a bigger plan to unpack.

I don't know why our baby had to go back up to heaven, but Daddy says maybe I'll understand more when I'm seventy-seven.

God brought you to Mommy's tummy for a reason; it's true. But that doesn't mean that I don't really miss you.

But for now, I'll keep you safe in my heart until the day that we will never have to be apart.

I'll look up to heaven and blow you a kiss because I know that God has a plan for this.

ABOUT THE AUTHOR

Amanda McKinney is a hometown elementary teacher, a former foster parent, a football coach's wife, a mother of three boys, and now an author of the book *God Has a Plan for This*.

For close to a decade, she has served her community as an inspirational teacher known best for building community within her classroom and encouraging her students to grow academically, socially, and emotionally.

When she isn't in the classroom or chauffeuring her children around, you can often find Amanda supporting the local high school athletic teams as a coach's wife, serving at church with her family, or spending time with her four younger siblings and parents on the small cattle farm they grew up on.

Amanda and her husband, Tyler, have dealt with recurrent pregnancy loss for several years before and after adopting their three incredible children. As difficult as it is, Amanda uses this as a ministry opportunity to pour into other people's lives and encourage them through what can, at times, feel like a very lonely journey.

Her hope as an author is that she can help at least one person through the grief they may be dealing with by losing a child of any age or development. If you are walking the streets of heartache, please know that you are not alone, and more than that, you are immensely loved.

CPSIA information can be obtained
at www.ICGtesting.com
Printed in the USA
BVHW011933190523
664484BV00008B/505